WHAT PEOPLE ARE SAYING ABOUT
Life Between the Bookends

"I enjoyed and was convicted by *Life Between the Bookends*. Thanks for sharing His heart."

– California

"I could not hold back the tears. This book presents exactly what the Body of Christ needs to hear."

– Arizona

"Jon, thank you for stirring me up to reconsider my priorities in life."

– Florida

"*Life Between the Bookends* is fresh air in a stale religious environment. I'm thankful the Lord put this message on your heart."

– Texas

Other Books By the Author

- *A Church Building Every 1/2 Mile: What Makes American Christianity Tick?*

- *What's With Paul & Women? Unlocking the Cultural Background to 1 Timothy 2*

- *No Will of My Own: How Patriarchy Smothers Female Dignity & Personhood*

- *Christ Minimized? A Response to Rob Bell's Love Wins*

- *The Pastor Has No Clothes: Moving from Clergy-Centered Church to Christ-Centered Ekklesia*

- *To Preach or Not to Preach? The Church's Urgent Question* (David C. Norrington with Replies to the Critics & an Introduction by Jon Zens)

- *58 to 0: How Christ Leads Through the One Anothers*

- *Jesus Is Family: His Life Together*

Available online at: www.JonZens.com

Life Between the Bookends

Is the Lord's Passion Our Passion Too?

JON ZENS

All rights reserved. No part of this book may be used or reproduced, stored in a retrieval system, or transmitted in any form or by any means, electronic, mechanical, photocopying, recording, scanning, or otherwise, without written permission from the publisher except in the case of brief quotations embodied in critical articles and reviews. Permission for wider usage of this material can be obtained through Quoir by emailing permission@quoir.com.

Copyright © 2018 by Jon Zens.

First Edition

Cover artwork: Dotty Zens
Cover design and layout: Rafael Polendo (polendo.net)

Biblical citations are taken from the *The New American Standard Bible*, modified by Jon Zens, and *The New Living Translation*, modified by Jon Zens.

ISBN 978-1-938480-28-7

This volume is printed on acid free paper and meets ANSI Z39.48 standards.

Printed in the United States of America

Published by Quoir
Orange, California

www.quoir.com

Table of Contents

Life Between the Bookends 6

Endnote 31

For Further Reflection 34

LIFE BETWEEN THE BOOKENDS

Is the Lord's Passion Our Passion Too?

If a rocket launched to the moon is off by *one degree*, it will miss the moon by 4,000 miles. Something akin to this has happened in terms of how most people are pursuing life. Their sights are off-kilter and as a result they are missing what is really important by more than 4,000 miles, figuratively speaking.

This is aptly illustrated in what occurred in the futuristic film, *Brazil* (1985). A low-level government employee swats a fly that lands in the printer, resulting in the wrong name being printed on a bureaucratic form—Archibald Buttle instead of Archibald Tuttle. This sets off a domino-effect of misdirected events, including the death of Mr. Buttle. One letter in a name being botched resulted in false assumptions and mass confusion.

Likewise, as we will see, the Lord's purpose at the beginning and end of history is a Bride and a Groom. But, it is as if a letter has been changed, and—because of many factors—people end up living as if God desires a "bridge" for His Son instead of a Bride. So, armed with this incorrect assumption, they expend energy building bridges of all sorts for the Son. They are well-intentioned, but ill-informed.

The truth is, every human being is on a journey. Some journeys are filled with landmines and obstacles, while others seem to move along seamlessly. The paths of multitudes are leading them to a deep feeling of loneliness. They then embark on

> an intense search for the experience of unity and community...to ask anew how love, friendship, brotherhood and sisterhood can free them from isolation and offer them a sense of intimacy and belonging. All around us we see the many ways by which the people of the Western world are trying to escape this loneliness (Henry Nouwen).

I would ask you to consider these vital questions: What drives your heart in life, and have you considered what passion fuels God's heart? I would like to explore with you a burden I carry: Are our hearts in step with the Lord's heart? Have we been deceived into seeking bridges instead of the Bride?

THE BOOKENDS

Is it possible for us to know what is central in the Lord's purposes? I would suggest that it is crystal clear what the Lord is after. His purpose is revealed and confirmed by the first two chapters of Genesis and the last two chapters of Revelation—the *Bookends* of Scripture. The Bookends clearly show that pre-history, history and post-history are all about a Bride and a Groom.

Genesis 1-2 and Revelation 21-22 are the only portions of the Bible where *sin is not present*. In Genesis 1-2 sin has not yet entered a pristine creation; in Revelation 21-22 sin has been eradicated in a New Heaven/New Earth. Death was announced as a possibility in Gen. 1-2; there is no more death in Rev. 21-22, only life in the Lamb.

Genesis 1 - 2

Although it was veiled at the time, the dominant image in Gen. 1-2 is *male and female*, a Groom and a Bride.

> Then God said, "Let Us make man in Our image, according to Our likeness; and let them rule over the fish of the sea and over the birds of the sky and over the cattle and over all the earth, and over every creeping thing that creeps on the earth." God created man in His own image, in the image of God He created him; *male and female* He created them.

We must understand that the Hebrew word for "man" is *Adam*, and that the woman is included in the meaning. Notice Genesis 5:1-2–

> This is the book of the generations of Adam. In the day when God created Adam, He made him in the likeness of God. He created them male and female, and He blessed them and named them 'Adam' in the day when they were created.

Even when Adam was 'alone,' Eve was inside of him. The Lord's goal was for the male to have a Bride. Consider the narrative that tells us how they met.

> Then the Lord God said, "It is not good for the man to be alone; I will make him a helper suitable for him." Out of the ground the Lord God formed every beast of the field

and every bird of the sky, and brought *them* to Adam to see what he would call them; and whatever Adam called a living creature, that was its name. The man gave names to all the cattle, and to the birds of the sky, and to every beast of the field, but for Adam there was not found a helper suitable for him. So the LORD God caused a deep sleep to fall upon the man, and he slept; then He opened his *pleura* and closed up the flesh at that place. The LORD God fashioned into a woman what He had taken from Adam, and brought her to the man. Adam said,

"This is now bone of my bones,
And flesh of my flesh; She shall be called Woman,
Because she was taken out of Adam."

For this reason a man shall leave his father and his mother, and be joined to his wife; and they shall become one flesh. And the man and his wife were both naked and were not ashamed.

Note that there was something much greater going on here than just the beginning of "marriage." What was the Lord's perspective of this union of male and female in the Genesis account? Paul revealed this to us in Ephesians 5:29-32.

For no one ever hated his own flesh, but nourishes and cherishes it, just as Christ also *does* the *ekklesia*,* because we are members of His body. FOR THIS REASON A MAN SHALL LEAVE HIS FATHER AND MOTHER AND SHALL BE JOINED TO HIS WIFE, AND THE TWO SHALL BECOME ONE FLESH. This mystery is great; but I am speaking with reference to Christ and the *ekklesia*.

Adam and Eve were pictures of what would blossom in a distant fullness of time when Christ would leave His Father in heaven and purchase the *ekklesia* of God with His own blood on the cross in AD 33.

When the time came for God to bring Eve forth from Adam, He caused a deep sleep to come upon Adam, and then opened his *pleura* in order to fashion the woman. Likewise, Christ in His crucifixion experienced the sleep of death, and His *pleura* was opened by the soldier's spear to give birth to His Bride, the *ekklesia*.

After Adam and Eve sinned, the Lord put into motion the fulfillment of His promise that came to Eve in the words to the serpent:

> And I will put enmity
> Between you and the woman,
> And between your seed and her seed;
> He shall bruise you on the head,
> And you shall bruise him on the heel."

Through her, One will come who will crush the head of the serpent. From that point on there is a lineage within humanity leading to the birth of Christ through both Mary, and step-father Joseph.

All of creation was brought into existence by Christ. When Adam was formed, it was about Christ. When Eve was fashioned, it was about Christ's wife. All things are by Him, to Him, through Him and for Him. The heartthrob of Gen. 1-2 is the Bride being brought to the Groom. As Paul noted, this is a great mystery, but it is all about Jesus and His Bride. If we do not get this, we will miss the moon by 4,000 miles.

Revelation 21-22

Just as Gen. 1-2 began with a creation which focused on an earth without sin, Rev. 21-22 tells of a New Heaven/New Earth where the curse of sin has been lifted. Also, as Gen. 1-2 unveiled a Bride for Adam, so Rev. 21-22 ends the story with the Last Adam, Christ, and His beautiful Bride. Listen to John's description of a flawless earth joined with heaven:

> Then I saw a new heaven and a new earth; for the first heaven and the first earth passed away, and there is no longer *any* sea. And I saw the holy city, new Jerusalem, coming down out of heaven from God, made ready as a *Bride adorned for her husband.* And I heard a loud voice from the throne, saying, "Behold, the tabernacle of God is among humans, and He will dwell among them, and they shall be His people, and God Himself will be among them, and He will wipe away every tear from their eyes; and there will no longer be *any* death; there will no longer be *any* mourning, or crying, or pain; the first things have passed away"…Then one of the seven angels who had the seven bowls full of the seven last plagues came and spoke with me, saying, "Come here, *I will show you the Bride, the wife of the Lamb*"…I saw no temple in it, for the Lord God the Almighty and the Lamb are its temple. And the city has no need of the sun or of the moon to shine on it, for the glory of God has illumined it, and its lamp *is* the Lamb…Then he showed me a river of the water

of life, clear as crystal, coming from the throne of God and of the Lamb, in the middle of its street. On either side of the river was the tree of life, bearing twelve *kinds of* fruit, yielding its fruit every month; and the leaves of the tree were for the healing of the nations. There will no longer be any curse; and the throne of God and of the Lamb will be in it, and His bond-servants will serve Him; they will see His face, and His name *will be* on their foreheads. And there will no longer be *any* night; and they will not have need of the light of a lamp nor the light of the sun, because the Lord God will illumine them; and they will reign forever and ever…The Spirit and the Bride say, "Come." And let the one who hears say, "Come." And let the one who is thirsty come; let the one who wishes take the water of life without cost.

Peter mentioned this in his second letter. He spoke of scoffers, and the days of old when "the world at that time was destroyed, being flooded with water. But by His word the present heavens and earth are being reserved for fire, kept for the day of judgment and destruction of ungodly people…But according to His promise we are looking for new heavens and a new earth, where righteousness dwells."

The Beginning and the End

Having observed quite clearly the overwhelming emphasis on the Bride-Groom theme in Gen. 1-2 and Rev. 21-22, we are able to rightly discern the Lord's heart. All of history is about Jesus Christ obtaining a Bride out of every people-group on earth.

Obviously, Jesus' heart is parallel with His Father's desires. How did Jesus express His singular purpose? "I will build my *ekklesia* and the gates of death will not prevail against it." Paul stated in Ephesians 1:22-23 that Christ guides and directs all things with reference to the apple of His eye, the *ekklesia*:

> God has put all things under the authority of Christ and has made him head over all things for the benefit of the *ekklesia*. And the *ekklesia* is his body; it is made full and complete by Christ, who fills all things everywhere with himself. (*NLT*)

Are We in Step with Jesus' Heart?

As we look at the Bookends of Scripture, it is clear what is on the hearts of Jesus and His Father: the realization of a Bride for the Son to pour His love into, and a Groom for the Bride to pour her love into.

What does it mean to be a "person after God's own heart"? Well, in Acts 13:22 we read, "God testified concerning [David]: 'I have found David son of Jesse, a man after my own heart; he will do everything I want him to do.'" Apparently, a huge part of David being in line with God's heart was his fervor for the "Lord's house." He wanted to see a dwelling place for his God. David confessed to the prophet Nathan, "Here I am living in a palace of cedar while the Lord has no resting place." On another occasion, David's passion was expressed like this:

> "I will not enter my house

>   or go to my bed,
> I will allow no sleep to my eyes
>   or slumber to my eyelids,
> till I find a place for the LORD,
>   a dwelling for the Mighty One of Jacob."

When David spoke of the "Lord's house" or His "dwelling place," he did have in view a physical structure. However, the temple that was ultimately built by Solomon was a type and shadow of what would come later—Christ as the temple and His Bride as His dwelling place. In Hebrews 3, believers are called "Christ's house."

Putting David's heart-cry into New Covenant perspective, then, would mean that our passion should be to pour out our lives—our talents, our time, our resources—into the house Jesus is building, His *ekklesia*. This entails an *organic, living Bride expressing Christ on earth through relational face-to-face communities*, not outward churchy items like buildings, programs, pulpits, prominent leaders and tithing. Many associate "God's house" with a structure having pews, but in reality it is a group of Brides gathering around their Bridegroom, Jesus Christ.

Our passions in life cannot be hidden. In light of David's zeal, we should ask ourselves, "Are our passions in line with the Lord's heart as revealed in the Bookends?" and "Are we willing to be homeless and sleepless until the Lord has a home where His Son is welcome?"

Of course, we should expect Jesus to live out His Father's passion, and indeed we find an example of this in John 2.

The Jewish leaders had turned the Temple into a religious Wal-Mart, and He overturned their cash registers. In the midst of this scene we read, "His disciples remembered that it was written, 'ZEAL FOR YOUR HOUSE WILL CONSUME ME.'" Jesus cared about His Father's place, knowing that He would become The Temple, and that His Bride would make up the living stones of the New Jerusalem.

THE FORGOTTEN BRIDEGROOM?

It has become increasingly clear to me that few people connect the word "Bridegroom" with Jesus. Yet, in light of the centrality of this image in Gen. 1-2 and Rev. 21-22, this is surely a tragedy. If you check out the posters that present the names of Christ, you will find that "Bridegroom" is rarely listed.

From the outset, Jesus is revealed as a *Bridegroom* in John's Gospel.

- John 1—"In the beginning…" A new creation is now begun by the One who brought the first creation into existence.

- "There came a man sent from God, John." The forerunner is a friend of the Bridegroom, as we will see.

- "The Word was made flesh." A new Adam is incarnated. And just as it was said of the first Adam—"it is not good for him to be alone"—now it can be said of the Last Adam—"it is not good for Him to be alone." He needs a Bride.

- John 1:47—Another theme is introduced, a new Jacob. Jesus chooses twelve disciples, just as Jacob had twelve sons. (This helps us understand why twelve men were chosen. 'Apostle' is not solely a male function; we know from Romans 16 that Junia was an 'apostle'.) Jesus says to Nathaniel, "you are an Israelite in whom is no guile" [unlike Jacob] and "you shall see the heaven opened and the angels of God ascending and descending on the Son of Man" (1:51), echoing Jacob's experience in Genesis 28.

- John 2—Jesus as the Bridegroom-to-be attends a couple's wedding in Cana. He takes living water and turns it into wine, and takes away the shame the groom faced for running out of wine. Jesus' wine is the absolute best. But He is not just attending a festive wedding. Christ connects this first "sign" with the "hour" of His death. The wine symbolizes the blood of His death in which He gave His last breath for the life of His Bride. The wine at the Last Supper pointed to the great wedding supper of the Lamb and His Bride.

- John 3:29—"The Bride belongs to the Bridegroom. The friend who attends the Bridegroom waits and listens for Him, and is full of joy when he hears the Bridegroom's voice. This joy is mine and is now complete." Now we have a Groom, a friend of the Groom—but where is the Bride?

- John 4—The new Jacob finds a new Rachel at a well—at noon.
    - Isaac's wife was found at a well (Gen 24)
    - Jacob comes to a well and Rachel appears at noon
    - Moses came to a well and found a Bride, Zipporah (Exodus 2)

- The Bridegroom, Christ, figuratively speaking, finds His Bride at a well. Jesus is weary from His journey and asks for her water; she is weary from life's journey and asks for His water. The Samaritan woman is a perfect picture of Christ's Bride—she is one woman, but she is part Jewish and part Gentile. The real Bride/Groom and wedding feast are unveiled in Revelation 21-22—believers from every tribe, kindred and tongue are joined forever with Christ in the New Heaven/New Earth.

Why?

The Bookends of Scripture are clear that the Bride/Groom theme is central in the purpose of God. You might ask, then, "What is behind the Son having a Bride? Why is this so important?"

We can certainly say that Paul saw the Lord's hand as guiding all things with reference to a specific goal:

> We have obtained an inheritance, having been predestined according to His purpose who works all things after the counsel of His will, to the end that we who were the first to hope in Christ would be to the praise of His glory. To me, the very least of all saints, this grace was given, to preach to the Gentiles the unfathomable riches of Christ, and to bring to light what is the administration of the mystery which for ages has been hidden in God who created all things; so that the manifold wisdom of God might now be made known through the *ekklesia* to the rulers and the authorities in the heavenly *places. This was* in accordance with the eternal purpose which He carried out in Christ Jesus our Lord…

When boiled down, the Groom and the Bride are about *love and relationship* flowing from Father, Son and Spirit. Before time, the Father was pouring His love into the Son, the Son pouring His love into the Father, and the Spirit pouring out His love among them. It was purposed that this fellowship should expand, and the Son, being "alone" in some profound sense, would obtain a Bride (as did Adam). He would then pour His love into His wife, and the Bride would, in grateful response, pour her love into her Husband.

Adrienne von Speyr in 1948 captured a taste of the depths of this interplay of love:

> The measure of this love is His own: *As I have loved you, you should love one another.* His love for us sprang from His love for the Father. Out of precisely the same love, we

should love each other: a wholly pure love, which comes through the Son from the Father; a love having the same characteristics as the Son's love for the Father and that is, therefore, extravagant. The love the Son receives from the Father and returns to Him is a totally burning, giving, poured out, consumed love.

Frank Viola in 2009 expressed it like this in *From Eternity to Here*:

> It is as if the Father said: "It is not good for you to be alone, my Son. I will make for you a companion who corresponds to you. One like you, but not you. I will give you one upon whom you can pour out the passion of your being. But there is only one way I can accomplish this task. I must remove a part of yourself out of yourself and build another you. And you will no longer be one. There will be another, a she. She will be you in another form. She shall be the object of your unbridled passion. You shall be her *Lover*, and she will be your *beloved*. Indeed, she shall reciprocate your own passion, just as you reciprocate my passion."

As Jesus was about to depart physically from His disciples, we are told:

> Now before the Feast of the Passover, Jesus knowing that His hour had come that He would depart out of this world to the Father, having loved His own who were in the world, He loved them to the end.

In His love to them as His end approached, He gave them these words:

> He who has seen Me has seen the Father; how *can* you say, 'Show us the Father'? Do you not believe that I am in the Father, and the Father is in Me? The words that I say to

you I do not speak on My own initiative, but the Father abiding in Me does His works. Believe Me that I am in the Father and the Father is in Me; otherwise believe because of the works themselves.

In that day you will know that I am in My Father, and you in Me, and I in you.

Now, Father, glorify Me together with Yourself, with the glory which I had with You before the world was.

That they may all be one; even as You, Father, *are* in Me and I in You, that they also may be in Us, so that the world may believe that You sent Me.

Father, I desire that they also, whom You have given Me, be with Me where I am, so that they may see My glory which You have given Me, for You loved Me before the foundation of the world.

I have made Your name known to them, and will make it known, so that the love with which You loved Me may be in them, and I in them.

Jesus returned to the Father after His resurrection. Forty days later as He promised—"I will come to you"—Jesus came to His Bride on the Day of Pentecost in the person of the Holy Spirit. She, the *ekklesia*, continues the ministry of Christ on earth by loving Him, expressing Him, loving the brothers and sisters, and being a healing presence for the nations.

The eternal purpose in Christ is all about the interplay of love flowing from Father, Son, Spirit and the Bride.

Made for Love

We must remember that humans were created as the image of God. Because of this they are wired for relationships—with the Lord and with people. Tragically, however, sin has ill-effected human relationships at all levels. Nevertheless, as Frank Viola pointed out:

> Every love story that the minds of mortal men and women construct, every love story that has made its appearance in the pages of human history—whether fiction or nonfiction—is but a reflection, a pale image, a faint portrait, a scrambled version of the sacred romance of the ages.

That sacred romance, of course, is unfolded in the Bookends of the Bible—a Groom, a Bride and a wedding feast.

People can't escape relationships. Reflect on the 1000's of songs musicians and singers have created. Why do the bulk of them deal with aspects of "love" among people—the discovery of it, the bliss of it, the maintenance of it, the unfaithfulness/betrayal in it, and the ending of it? It is because humans are relational to the core. Consider several lyrics from popular songs.

> I know what it's like to be forgotten
> Left alone with your simple dreams
> But even dreams are fading fast
> No one to turn to when you can't sleep at night
> Waking up to another day that will soon be over
> And if you think that time has forgotten you
> Well just look into my eyes
> And know the times will change

(Hall & Oates, "Don't Hold Back Your Love")

When that boy leaves
And you need someone to turn to
When you feel alone
You will know you're not alone
If you've been true
To all who are true to you
You'll make it
You'll make it fine

(Joan Armatrading, "More Than One Kind of Love")

Most people are looking for love in all the wrong places. They are looking for that "final solution," and "look at a new friend, a new lover or a new community with Messianic expectations" in hopes that their loneliness will finally end (Henri Nouwen). But they should come and experience the love of the Bridegroom who never disappoints those who cast themselves on Him, and be a part of the fellowship of His Bride.

The Lord's Life or Our Life?

Based on the revelation found in the Bookends of Scripture, Genesis 1-2 and Revelation 21-22, it is clear enough what the heartthrob of our Lord is—a loving purpose to obtain a Bride for the Groom, with the result of love exuding among all the persons involved. Is the life that we now live on earth driven by, informed by and shaped by the love of God poured out in our hearts by the Spirit in light of God's eternal purpose in His Son?

How many words and pictures does the Lord have to use in order to show us His heart? By the revelation given at the beginning and end of history we know for sure what He is after. Are we willing to look at what we are doing with our lives in light of what we know He is doing to make His Son preeminent? Does the pervasive presence of the Bride, the Lamb and the coming wedding feast have an arresting impact on us?

A Game-Changer

For many, the opening up of the eternal purpose by the Spirit is a new beginning. This happened to Frank Viola in 1992. "All the sermons I heard since I was a child faded dead away…A page had turned. Suddenly everything became about Him and His ultimate purpose…I had read the Bible dozens of times, [but] I had missed the main point…The Lord's ageless purpose has given my very existence on this earth new meaning and direction. To put it another way, in beholding God's central purpose, I found my own purpose. In touching His ultimate passion, I found my own passion." I pray this Spirit-revelation will be your portion, if it is not already.

The Lord Draws the Lines

Remember, God defines what is real, not us. What is His reality? His reality is working all things in history toward the goal of the Son having a people into which He pours out His love, and a Bride who pours out her love to Him who gave Himself for her. Is our daily living aligned with this reality? Are we concerned that His reality (His Son) be our reality? As Paul put it so beautifully and compellingly:

> For the love of Christ controls us, having concluded this, that one died for all, therefore all died; and He died for all, so that they who live might no longer live for themselves, but for Him who died and rose again on their behalf.

THE VISION FADES

I have watched over the years as some who were in one season of their lives gripped by the Lord in His eternal purpose, for various reasons drifted away from it as time elapsed. As Bruce Springsteen pointed out in one of his songs:

> Now the hardness of this world slowly grinds your dreams away
> Makin' a fool's joke out of the promises we make
> And what once seemed black and white turns to so many shades of gray
> We lose ourselves in work to do and bills to pay
>
> ("Blood Brothers")

Paul was diligent and vigilant to keep his stewardship of the mystery in front of his eyes. When he awoke every morning—often in hunger, having been beaten or pelted with rocks—the love of Christ constrained him to keep himself in line with Jesus' stated purpose to build His *ekklesia*, the Bride. I trust that you will not be diverted from what is unfurled in the Bookends of the Bible.

Is It Jesus or About Jesus?

Looking over the religious landscape, it seems to me that Jesus is used as a front for many evangelical/fundamentalist ministries and programs that in fact have virtually nothing to do with God's passion for the Son and His Bride. It is like we are mindlessly expending time, energy and resources chasing "it's" and "things" about Christ, instead of pursuing the Son and His Bride. Frank Viola cracks the nut by saying:

> All of the churches and movements I was involved in had effectively preached to me an "it." Evangelism is an "it." The power of God is an "it." Eschatology is an "it." Christian theology is an "it." Christian doctrine is an "it." Faith is an "it." Apologetics is an "it." Healing and deliverance are "its."
>
> I made the striking discovery that I don't need an "it." I have never needed an "it." And I will never need an "it." Christian "its," no matter how good or true, eventually wear out, run dry, and become tiresome.
>
> I don't need an "it," I need a Him!
>
> And so do you.
>
> We do not need "things." We need Jesus Christ.
>
> You can chase spiritual things until you are blue in the face. And there will always be some Christian who is

peddling a new "it" or "thing" upon which to center your life. Warning: If you buy into it, you will most certainly miss Him.

When the Father gives us something, it's always His Son. When the Son gives us something, it's always Himself. This insight greatly simplifies the Christian life. Instead of seeking many spiritual things, we seek only Him. Our single occupation is the Lord Jesus Christ. He becomes our only pursuit. We do not seek divine things; we seek a divine person. We do not seek gifts; we seek the giver who embodies all the gifts. We do not seek truth; we seek the incarnation of all truth.

(*From Eternity to Here*)

The Now or the Eternal Purpose?

As I said at the outset, too many people are very busy filling their life with activities that eat up their time and money, but they have not taken the time to consider, "What is driving the Lord's loving heart?" Don't we want our brief lives on earth to be in step with His passion as unfolded in the Bookends of Scripture? Aren't most approaches to life focused on the moment and the immediate future, and not on the big picture seen through God's eyes?

A Lesser End

"Man's chief end is to glorify God, and to enjoy him forever" (*Westminster Shorter Catechism*, 1646).

This statement certainly has some truth in it, but does it reflect sensitivity to the "chief end" of the Lord? Isn't it *individualistic*, not looking at His purpose for the Son to have a family? This illustrates how easy it is for people to construct a worldview without giving heed to God's intentions in the Son.

Someone Has to Pay a Price

There is no way around the fact that giving oneself to the eternal purpose will involve a cost and sacrifice. Paul certainly knew this well, as he bore the marks of the Lord Jesus on his body. These two stories Christ shared underscore that there are serious implications in pursuing His kingdom.

> The kingdom of heaven is like a treasure hidden in the field, which a person found and hid *again*; and from joy over it they go and sell all that they have and buy that field.

> Again, the kingdom of heaven is like a merchant seeking fine pearls, and upon finding one pearl of great value, he went and sold all that he had and bought it.

Someone has to sacrifice in order for the Kingdom to be a reality. There is an attraction and value that is integral to Christ and His purposes that would cause people to part with their belongings in order to cast their lot in with Him. Does this description correspond to the longings of your heart?

With the Masses or With the Remnant?

In the history since Cain and Abel that led to the fullness of time and the incarnation of Christ, those living by faith have always been found in a *remnant*, a small part of the whole. To mention a few, think of the remnant in Noah's time when the flood came, in Lot's time when Sodom was destroyed, in Caleb and Joshua's time, in Elijah's time, and in Christ's time only a few in Israel were waiting to receive the Messiah.

Since roughly AD 200 to the present there has always been a remnant holding on to Christ, while the religious masses have found themselves enslaved to a formalized institutional system almost void of life in the Spirit.

You have a choice to make. Are you going to go along with the masses in status quo religion, or be a part of the remnant who are living out the life of Christ in light of the Bookends? Are you going to allow the human forces whose traditions have clouded and muddied the eternal purpose in Christ keep you from pursuing the Lamb and His Bride?

Eugene Peterson believes that a remnant is most likely to impact our wounded world:

> "[I came to] a developing conviction that the most effective strategy for change, for revolution—at least on the large scale that the Kingdom of God involves—comes from a minority working from the margins...that a minority people working from the margins has the best chance of being a community capable of penetrating the non-community, the mob, the depersonalized, function-defined

crowd that is the sociological norm of America" (*The Pastor: A Memoir*, p.16).

I appeal to you: stand fast in proclaiming and living out the message of the Bookends— "For this reason a man shall leave his father and mother and shall be joined to his wife, and the two shall become one flesh.' This mystery is great; but I am speaking with reference to Christ and the *ekklesia*."

The Bookends demonstrate clearly what is important to the Lord. Is what they reveal important to us? If the increase of His loving purpose resonates in our hearts, then we do well to pour out our love to the Son of God and His Bride!

"His disciples remembered that it was written, 'Zeal for Your house will consume me.'" Does Jesus' zeal burn in your soul? Are we consumed with desires to see His house prosper and be enlarged?

Endnote

*You may not be familiar with the word *ekklesia*. I have used this word throughout this book instead of "church." Here's why, based on excerpts from Chapter 5 of *Jesus Is Family*:

> The tragedy is that most people's assumptions about "church" are false, and the truth is buried in the cemetery behind the church building.
>
> "Church" is the English word used in most versions of the Bible to translate the Greek word *ekklesia*. For example, Jesus said, "I will build My *ekklesia* . . ." Most English Bibles rendered this, "I will build My church." The truth is, "church" is a terrible translation of *ekklesia*.
>
> You can Google "church or ekklesia?" and find out why "church" is manifestly inappropriate. But here is a concrete illustration of a serious problem. When Tyndale's English translation of the New Testament appeared in 1526, he correctly rendered *ekklesia* as "congregation" or "assembly." But on two occasions, Acts 14:13 and 19:37, he translated *ekklesia* as *churche* because it referred to pagan places of worship. Isn't that fascinating?

Out of the 115 times *ekklesia* occurs in the NT, the King James Version rendered it "church" 112 times. Three times, Acts 19:32, 39, 41, it translated it as "congregation," because a non-Christian gathering was in view. Isn't that interesting!

Jesus said He is building "My *ekklesia*," not "church." Jesus' disciples would have been familiar with this word in two ways.

First, it was used in the Greek translation of the Old Testament (called the *Septuagint*) to translate the Hebrew word *Qahal*. This referred to the Israelites *as assembled together*, often before the Lord.

Secondly, *ekklesia* was commonly used in the civil realm and had in view *a duly assembled group of citizens who came together to discuss and take care of common concerns in the community.*

Thus, this word primarily had both a spiritual and civil usage in the first century. Out of many choices, Jesus selected this word to define His building project. He used *ekklesia* three times in Matthew, once in chapter 16, and twice in chapter 18. In light of all the revealed dimensions, *ekklesia* must be defined as *the Lord's people gathered together to carry out the whole gamut of Christ's kingdom purposes…*

You can do "church" without *ekklesia* being present. "Church" can be carried out without commitment to anything beyond going to a building, singing some songs, putting some money in the plate, and listening to a sermon…

Ekklesia is the life of Christ flowing through the saints to carry out His purposes. There's a whole lot of "church" going on, but how much *ekklesia life* is really occurring?

For Further Reflection

1. Steve Carpenter, "Portraits of the Bridegroom in John/Revelation," #2, John Knox Seminary, January, 2006.

2. Heather Kendall, *The Tale of Two Kingdoms*, Essence Publishing, 2006, 448 pages.

3. Henri Nouwen, *Reaching Out*, Harper, 1977.

4. Milt Rodriguez, *The Community Life of God*.

5. T. Austin-Sparks, *The Watchword of the Son of Man*.

6. Kendra Haloviak Valentine, "The Wedding at the Well," *Ministry*, January, 2014, pp. 16-19.

7. Adreinne von Speyr, *The Farewell Discourses, Meditations on John 13-17* [1948], *John*, Vol.3, Ignatius Press, 1987, 378 pages.

8. Frank Viola, *From Eternity to Here*, David Cook, 2009, 315 pages.

9. Jon Zens, *Jesus Is Family: His Life Together*, 2017.

10. Jon Zens, "Life Between the Bookends," YouTube.

11. Jon Zens, "The Tucson Videos—2016," #1–#17, YouTube.

Jon may be reached at:

jzens@searchingtogether.org

(715) 338–2796

P.O. Box 548
St Croix Falls, WI 54024

Many voices. One message.

Quoir is a boutique publishing company
with a single message: Christ is all.
Our books explore both His
cosmic nature and corporate expression.

For more information, please visit
www.quoir.com

www.ingramcontent.com/pod-product-compliance
Lightning Source LLC
Chambersburg PA
CBHW071550080526
44588CB00011B/1855